THE AWESOME KIDS GUIDE TO RACE

Written by Shayla Reese Griffin

Illustrated by Christina O.

Justice Leaders PRESS

For our babies

A Note to Readers
This book is about race in the United States of America. If it were written by someone living in a different country, or at a different time, it would be a different story, but a lot would be the same.

This is a book about **race**—how we group people based on where our ancestors were from.

It's about **racism**—how some racial groups have been treated unfairly.

And it's about **racial justice**—how awesome activists like you and me can work together to make sure everyone is treated equally.

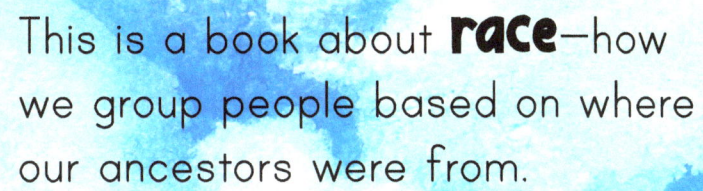
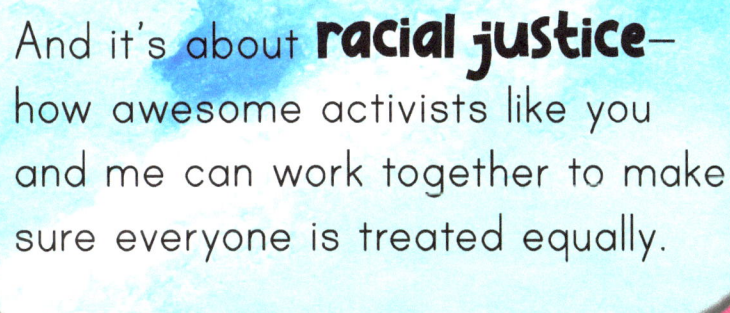

Then we began moving to different places.

Hundreds of thousands of years ago, all people lived on the continent of Africa.

We started to look a little bit different (not that different).

Did You Know?
99.9% of our DNA is exactly the same as every other person's on earth!

Fun Fact!
Humans have different skin colors because of the sun! Closer to the equator where people got a lot of sun, darker skin provided protection. In places with less sun, lighter skin helped people absorb enough Vitamin D.

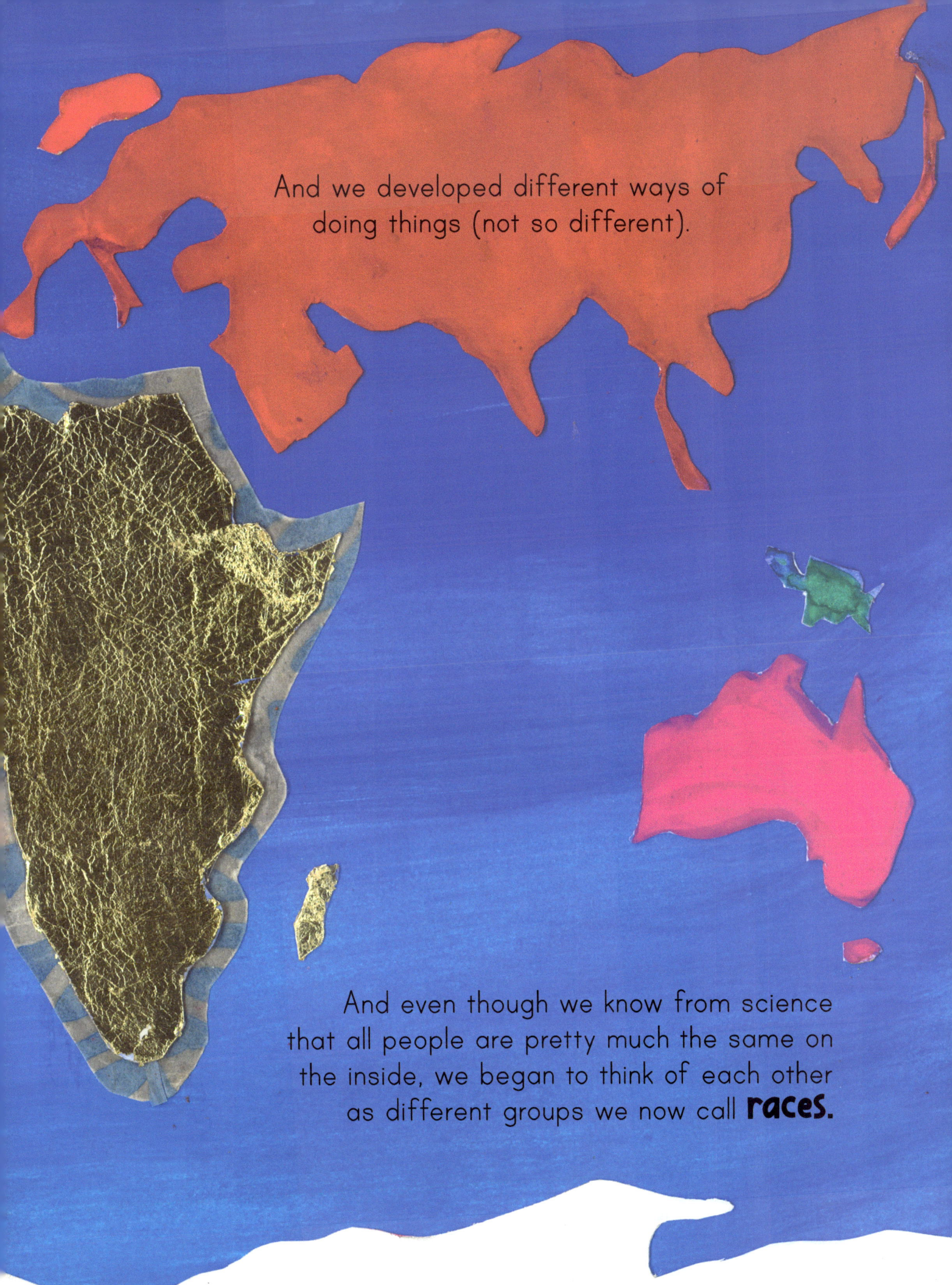

And we developed different ways of doing things (not so different).

And even though we know from science that all people are pretty much the same on the inside, we began to think of each other as different groups we now call **races.**

Our race is mostly based on where our biological grandparents', grandparents', grandparents', grandparents', grandparents', grandparents were from. We call these people our **ancestors.**

Some of us know where our ancestors were from. Some of us don't.

Some families are made up of people of the same race. Some families aren't.

Sometimes you can tell a person's race by looking at them. Sometimes you can't.

Some of the ways we group people by race will stay the same over time and place. Often, they won't.

Did You Know?
Race is a very confusing idea that people made up. It keeps changing and often doesn't make much sense. Don't worry, most adults are pretty confused about race too!

Within each racial group there are people who have different skin tones, hair textures, and hair colors,

who have different interests and abilities,

who speak different languages and are from different countries,

who are part of different ethnic groups, cultures, and religions,

and who are awesome **activists** working to change the world!

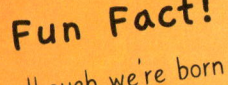

Fun Fact!

Even though we're born with lots of different hair colors, all of our hair begins turning gray or white as we age.

Did You Know?

All of these people identify as Black even though they look pretty different!

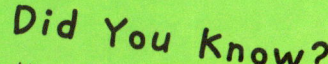

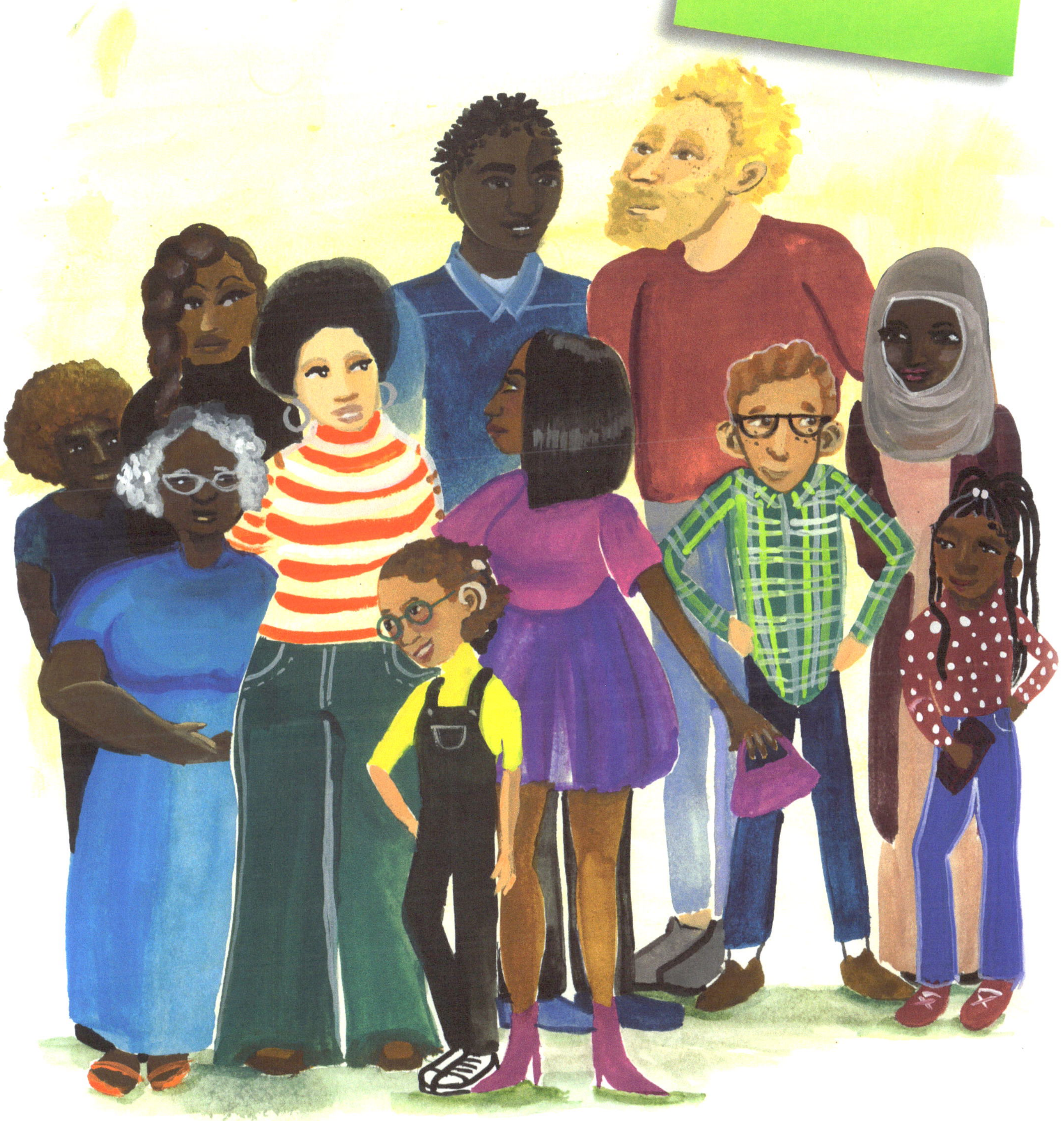

Some people in the United States are

Black

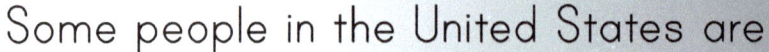

Black means a long long time ago your ancestors stayed in Africa as others moved to different parts of the world.

Dr. Wangari Maathai was an awesome activist from Kenya. She planted millions of trees to care for the earth.

Fun Fact!
The Dogon people of Mali were some of the world's first astronomers!

Did You Know?
Today, Black people live all over the world. Black people in the United States are sometimes called African American or Black American.

Did You Know?
The ancestors of some Black Americans lived in other countries outside of the continent of Africa—like Jamaica and St. Vincent—before coming to the United States.

Some people in the United States are

Indigenous

Indigenous American means a long long time ago your ancestors were the first people in North and South America.

Did You Know?
The Iroquois Confederacy is one of the oldest democracies on earth and inspired parts of the U.S. Constitution!

Fun Fact!
In North America, Indigenous people are often called Native American, First Nations, American Indian, Alaska Native, or by the name of their specific tribe or nation.

Elouise "Yellow Bird Woman" Cobell

was an awesome activist from the Blackfeet Nation.
She worked to get Indigenous Americans millions of
dollars the U.S. government owed them.

Did You Know?
Around 1100 CE the city of
Cahokia—near present day St.
Louis, Missouri—was as large
and technologically advanced as
any city in the world!

Some people in the United States are

Asian

Asian means a long long time ago your ancestors lived in Asia.

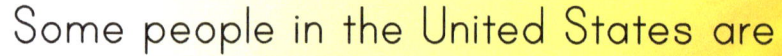

Fun Fact!

Asia is huge! It has more land and more people than any other continent on earth!

Fun Fact!

People from China invented the first fireworks in the world!

Dr. Durgabai Deshmukh
was an awesome activist from India. She was a lawyer who created programs to take care of children and families.

Did You Know?
Sometimes we use terms like South Asian to refer to people from specific regions.

Some people in the United States are

Pacific Islander

Pacific Islander means a long long time ago your ancestors lived on islands in the Pacific Ocean.

Fun Fact!

There are thousands of islands in the Pacific Ocean! The biggest is Australia. Together, Australia and the Pacific Islands are referred to as Oceania.

Did You Know?

People from Oceania were some of the first people on the planet to cross oceans!

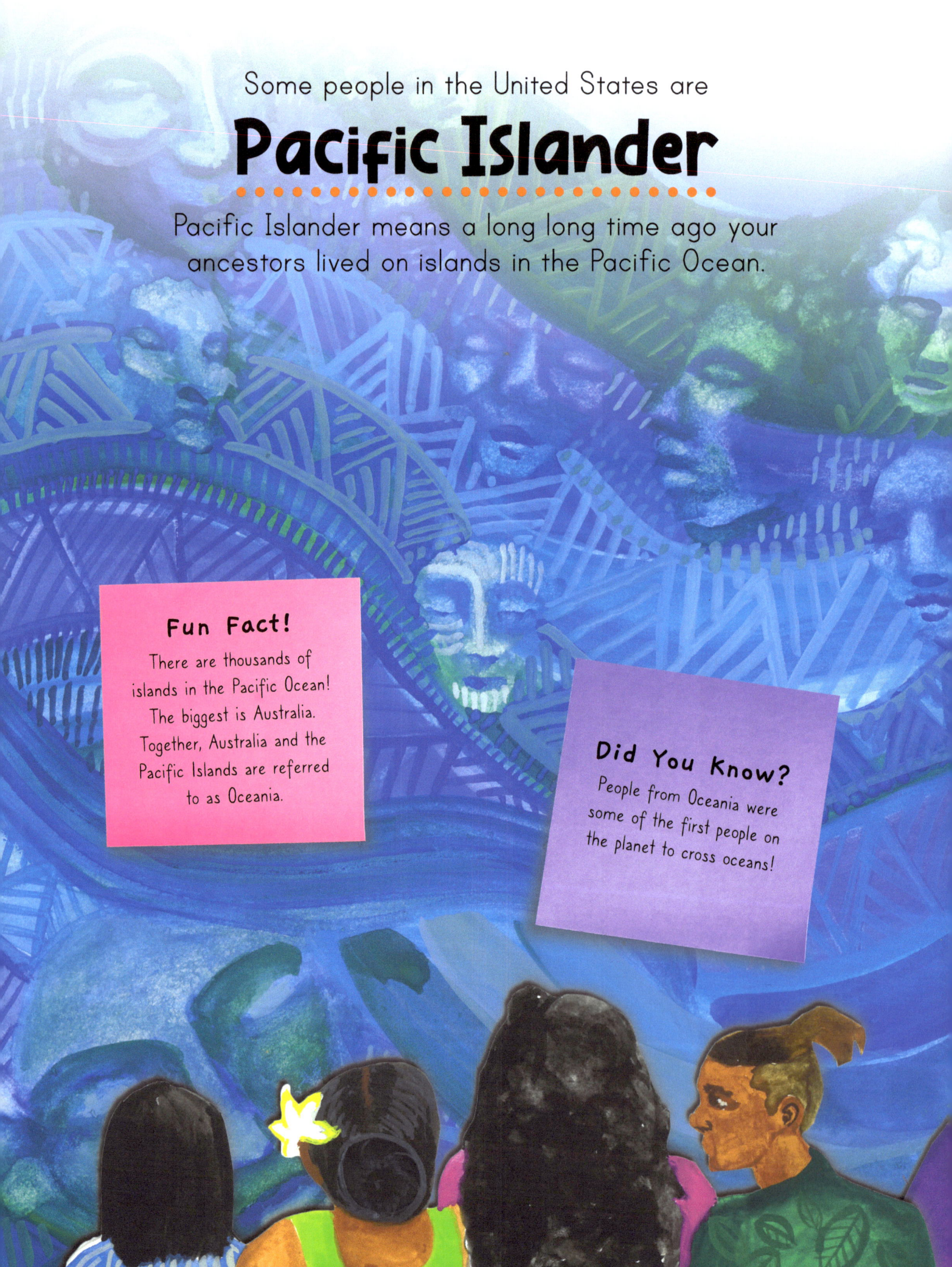

Dr. Hilda Heine

is an awesome activist who was the first woman to be president of the Marshall Islands. She is working to address climate change.

Did You Know?

Racial categories change! We've only recently started considering Pacific Islander a racial group. And, it isn't clear where Indigenous Australians fit in.

Some people in the United States are

White

White means a long long time ago your ancestors
lived in Europe.

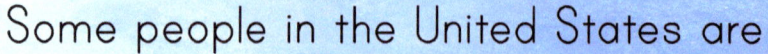

Joseph Sturge
was an awesome
activist from
England. He
fought to
end slavery.

Did You Know?
White people are sometimes called Caucasian, but since most White people do not have ancestors from the Caucasus Mountains, it's usually not an accurate term.

Fun Fact!
People from Greece invented the Olympics, a competition of the world's best athletes!

Some people in the United States are

Middle Eastern or North African (MENA)

MENA means a long long time ago your ancestors lived in Southwest Asia or North Africa.

Did You Know?
There isn't always agreement on which places and people should be considered part of the Middle East. Some people prefer the term SWANA—Southwest Asian or North African.

Fun Fact!
People from ancient Mesopotamia—centered in present day Iraq—invented some of the first written languages in the world!

Nazik al-'Abid

was an awesome activist from Syria. She fought for equal rights for women.

Did You Know?
Many people who are MENA identify as Arab American.

Some people in the United States are

Multiracial

Multiracial means you have parents of different races.

August Wilson was an awesome activist whose father was White from Germany and whose mother was Black from the United States. He wrote plays that helped people understand the lives of Black Americans.

Stacey Milbern

was an awesome activist whose mother was Asian from Korea and whose father was White from the United States. She worked to make sure LGBTQIA+ people and people with disabilities had equal rights.

Fun Fact!
Most of us are probably a little bit of a mix because each one of us has thousands of ancestors and there's a good chance they came from different places.

Did You Know?
Multiracial people sometimes use the terms Biracial or Mixed to describe themselves. Or, they may name their specific racial identities. Some identify with only one of their racial groups.

Some people in the United States are

Latine

Latine means a long time ago your ancestors lived in Mexico, Central America, South America, or some Caribbean Islands.

Rigoberta Menchú is an awesome activist from Guatemala. She won the Nobel Peace Prize for fighting for Indigenous rights across the globe.

Today, awesome people of every race
live together in the United States.

We got here in
different ways.

Some groups have
been here for as
long as humans can
remember.

Some chose to
come here to start
a new life.

Others were not
given a choice.

And we have had different experiences.

Some groups have been treated well. Others have not.

This is a sad part of the story...

For thousands and thousands of years, **Indigenous** people lived on the land we now call the United States of America.

Then, across the ocean, some **White** Europeans decided it was theirs to take.

These colonizers traveled to the Americas, killed millions of **Indigenous** people, and took their land.

They traveled to Africa and took millions of **Black** people to work the land.

They traveled across North America, the Pacific Ocean, and the Caribbean searching for more power.

Each decision they made to take just a bit more brought new people to these shores.

People of every race arrived with creativity, knowledge, innovation.

Then, together with those who were already here, they worked hard and built this nation!

But **White** leaders wouldn't share all that was made with everyone who helped make it.

For hundreds of years they used violence and passed laws to stop **Black, Indigenous,** and other People of Color, who were **Asian, Pacific Islander, Latine, MENA** and **Multiracial** from
protecting their own bodies,
caring for their own children,
speaking their native languages,
wearing their natural hair,

living where they wanted,
saying what they wanted,
marrying who they wanted,
worshiping how they wanted,

voting,
becoming citizens,
buying homes,
attending schools,
visiting doctors,
finding jobs,
shopping in stores,
eating in restaurants,

drinking clean water,
receiving fair trials,
earning fair wages,
and learning their history.

To justify their actions, they invented lies that **White** people were better than other racial groups.

But awesome activists of <u>every</u> race—Indigenous, Black, White, Latine, Multiracial, Asian, MENA, and Pacific Islander—knew these lies weren't true!

They fought back!

They led revolts!

They sat in!

They spoke up!

They boycotted!

They voted!

They marched!

And they passed new laws to make things more fair!

Even though these activists changed a lot, **racism** still exists today.

Some people think and say mean things about People of Color.

Others even hurt them.

Characters in books and TV shows are less likely to look like them.

Laws and authority figures can be unfair to them.

And they've had fewer opportunities to make money— which often means less for their kids, and their kids' kids.

↑

This is oppression.

As a result, White people often get stuff they didn't really earn—even if they aren't trying to be mean.

Many people think and say nicer things about them.

They're more likely to find characters in books and TV shows that look like them.

Laws and authority figures tend to treat them better.

And they've been given more opportunities to make money— which often means more for their kids, and their kids' kids.

↑

This is privilege.

Did You Know?
People with privilege who help make things more fair are called **allies**.

Racism hurts us all!

It makes it hard to feel good about ourselves.

It makes it hard to be friends with each other.

It makes it hard to work together to come up with the best ideas to solve big problems.

And it makes it hard to tell the truth.

Did You Know?
Sometimes racism is so deep inside of us we don't even know it's there. This is called **implicit** or **unconscious bias**.

Fortunately, lots of people like you and me are taking action to make sure all people, from all places, and all races, are treated fairly!

We call this being **antiracist** and it's our responsibility!

CHECKLIST FOR AWESOME ANTIRACIST KIDS (& GROWNUPS TOO!)

- ☐ 1. We are proud of who we are and help others feel proud of who they are.

- ☐ 2. We get to know each other instead of making assumptions based on a person's race.

- ☐ 3. We treat each other kindly—especially people who haven't been treated very kindly throughout our history.

- ☐ 4. We apologize when we do something hurtful, even if we didn't mean to.

- ☐ 5. We watch shows and read books about people from different racial groups.

- ☐ 6. We play with toys, games, and dolls that reflect the diversity of our world.

- ☐ 7. We ask grownups to vote for people who believe everyone should be treated fairly.

- ☐ 8. We tell the people who get elected to pass laws that make life better for us all.

- ☐ 9. We learn the truth about our history and try not to repeat the same mistakes.

- ☐ 10. And when we notice something racist, WE SPEAK UP!

We are **awesome activists!**

Our ancestors were from all over the world!

And we are working together for **racial justice!**

Shayla Reese Griffin, PhD, MSW is co-founder of Justice Leaders Collaborative, which provides social justice training, coaching, and resources for individuals, schools, and organizations; author of *Those Kids, Our Schools: Race and Reform in An American High School*; and co-author of *Race Dialogues: A Facilitator's Guide to Tackling the Elephant in the Classroom*. She is Black American and has a multiracial family that includes people who are Black, White, Indigenous, Multiracial, and Latina. She lives with her spouse and three children and gets her best ideas at 3 a.m.

Christina O. is a multidisciplinary artist who specializes in fine art, puppetry, wood burning, jewelry design, and illustration. She utilizes a variety of textures and materials along with more traditional mediums. Her art draws inspiration from her Afro-Latina roots, motherhood, the loved ones around her, social and political events, her travels abroad, and moments of self reflection. Christina O. has had her work printed on the pages of Pikchur. magazine, has been commissioned by Black Lives Matter, is a member of the international art society Kappa Pi, and has shown her work in various galleries on the East Coast. Her goal for the work she creates is that it will exude the depths of the human spirit and the rhythm of life.

Justice Leaders PRESS

Published in 2023 in the USA by Justice Leaders Press www.justiceleaderspress.com
Text Copyright @ 2023 Shayla Reese Griffin
Illustrations Copyright @ 2023 Christina O.
Book Design by Tori Griffin & Shayla Reese Griffin
Edited by David Dobbie
Contributions by Victoria L. Birch and Margarette Griffin

ISBN: 979-8-9886449-0-3
Library of Congress Control Number: 2023912257

If you enjoyed this book and want more from
Justice Leaders Press
please consider supporting our work!

· ·

☐ 1. Leave a great rating and review online!

☐ 2. Share our book with someone in your life!

☐ 3. Ask your local library or bookstore to carry
The Awesome Kids Guide to Race!

Want to be the first to learn about our newest books and workshops? Check out our website to join our mailing list!

Visit
www.JusticeLeadersPress.com
for more resources on how to talk to kids about race, merch, and free downloads!

www.ingramcontent.com/pod-product-compliance
Lightning Source LLC
Chambersburg PA
CBHW041619120626

46551CB00003B/499